**F**rom an idea by Lion, David Reed of Parb[...] this booklet introduces the walker to the [...] delights and charms of this corner of Sou[...] West Lancashire. The Lions and their fa[...] have had much pleasure in preparing an[...] checking the walks chosen and we hope you the reader, will have much pleasure in walking them.

Regrettably, some short stretches of the walks are on the roads and lanes. Many of them can be very busy, so great care must be taken, especially if walking with children or dogs. Always walk on the footpaths when one is available, otherwise walk in single file facing the oncoming traffic.

Many of the walks can be linked together to make a full day's walking.

The time indicated at the beginning of each walk, is for an easy pace, with plenty of time to stop and look at the view, or take a well earned rest. If you estimate 2 miles per hour, this will give you a good indication of the length of the walk.

Many of the walks pass through farm land, so please keep dogs on the lead and observe the country code. Remember that the countryside does change. A gate may be replaced by a stile, a path can be re-routed. Be patient should you find the route differing slightly.

In short, take nothing but photographs, leave nothing but footprints.

Any comments on the walks or any ideas for additions to the walks, or perhaps a wish to know more about the Lions and their work, please write to:

**The Lion President, Douglas Valley Lions,**
**c/o Newburgh Post Office,**
**Newburgh,**
**Nr. Wigan,**
**Lancs WN8**

# this book

*"Take nothing but photographs, leave nothing but footprints."*

# Who are the Lions?

**T**he International Association of Lions Clubs was formed 75 years ago, the prime aim of the Association is to serve the community in which the members live. The motto of the Association is "We Serve".

There are currently 1.4 million Lions in 41,908 Clubs in 180 Countries and geographic areas throughout the World.

Each Club raises funds for charitable causes and spends those monies as it chooses to benefit those members of society who are less fortunate than most. There are also International causes:-

- Natural Disasters
- Blindness
- Diabetes
- Drug Awareness

Each Club is free to donate to any of these international causes.

## WHO ARE DOUGLAS VALLEY LIONS?

Douglas Valley Lions Club was formed in 1970 and is one of the British and Irish Clubs.

The Club has boundaries with the Lions Clubs of Wigan, Chorley, Southport and Ormskirk.

Since its formation Douglas Valley Lions have raised over £200,000 which it has spent in some of the following ways.

**Locally**
Electric wheelchairs
Holidays for the disabled and disadvantaged
Costs of telephone/heating in cases of need
Pieces of hospital equipment
Basic household furniture
Drug awareness teaching packs for the Secondary and Primary Schools.

**Internationally**
Eye Camps in the Third World
The education of a Mallawi Student
Donations to the Lions International Disaster Funds

DOUGLAS VALLEY
LIONS

# Walking in Parbold

## South West Lancashire

Ormskirk Book & Art Shop
Ormskirk, Lancashire L39 2LS

**ACKNOWLEDGMENTS**

Many thanks to the Lions and their families who have prepared and checked the walks.
Also thanks to Jenny and Derek Ashcroft of the Ormskirk Bookshop who saw the wider sale of the book and who persuaded the Lions to walk further afield in S. W. Lancs.

Royalties for this book will be donated to the Charity Fund of the Douglas Valley Lions Club.
The Ormskirk Book and Art Shop will also donate a percentage to a charity of their choice.

# Contents

In addition to raising funds a vital part of the service activity of Lions is giving time serving the community.

Over the years members of Douglas Valley Lions Club have spent many hours:-

> Transporting elderly and infirm relatives to visit their relations in hospital
> Transporting disabled persons to social clubs
> Clearing and tidying gardens
> Decorating homes
> Assisting in local events

All the royalties from the sale of this publication will go towards the charity funds of Douglas Valley Lions Club.

Thank you and happy walking.

# MAP SYMBOLS

.......... **Path & Direction of Travel**

.......... **Farm Tracks/Roads**

.......... **Wooded Areas**

.......... **Roads**

.......... **Church - Buildings**

.......... **Park - Start**

.......... **Telephone**

# WALK 1

# The Windmill to Rookery Farm

Walk covered by:-
PATHFINDER MAPS
No 699 and 711

Start:-
MAP REFERENCE
491105 MAP 699,
WINDMILL PH
Next to the Canal.

Parking:-
Parbold side of Canal.

Time of Walk:-
Approx 2.5 hours.

Take the footpath on the same side of the canal as the Windmill, West, towards Newburgh. After 500 yards, where the canal narrows, turn left up a farm track to Ash Brow. Turn right uphill, cross the main road and take the Public Footpath through Derby House Riding Stables and paddock, making sure to keep to the left hand side of the hedge, cross a stream over short bridge. Turn immediately right and follow the edge of the field to a wood. Take the footpath into the wood, and after approx 400 yards, cross the stream over a footbridge and climb a steep bank into a field. Turn left and follow the edge of the field to the corner, where the footpath turns sharp right and emerges on Cobbs Brow Lane.

Turn left, and after 200 yards, take the footpath on the left. IF YOU COME TO A LINE OF BOULDERS OPPOSITE, YOU HAVE COME TOO FAR.

Walk along the edge of the field to a corner where a plank bridge crosses a stream. After crossing the stream, walk directly across a field to a farm track which should be followed to Higher Lane. Cross Higher Lane to take the farm road which leads you through Rookery Farm yard.

Follow the footpath through the left hand gate and then go over two stiles, bearing right at the large tree in a gully, to a third stile in the corner of a conifer hedge at the rear of the house.

Cross this stile and follow the track to Hillock Lane. Cross the lane and go over a stile adjacent to the gate. Proceed up the farm road and after a steep section, which is brick paved, go past old farm buildings to a stile on the left.

Cross the field to a line of trees, which are followed on the right to reach an area of marshy ground. Bear right over this to the far corner of the field which is fringed by a wood.

Cross the stile, and go through the wood and up a bank to waste ground, (site of an old mine). Follow the footpath left down hill, keeping to the left edge of the field, and crossing further stiles and a steep downhill section, to reach Lees Lane.

Turn left and within 140 yards, turn sharp right by farmhouse. Follow the well defined farm road for some 500 yards and at the end of a downhill section, where the farm road levels out, bear right and take the footpath leading to the bridge over the river Douglas to the canal bank. Turn left along the canal tow path back to the Windmill Public House.

# Walk 1 *The Windmill to Rookery Farm*

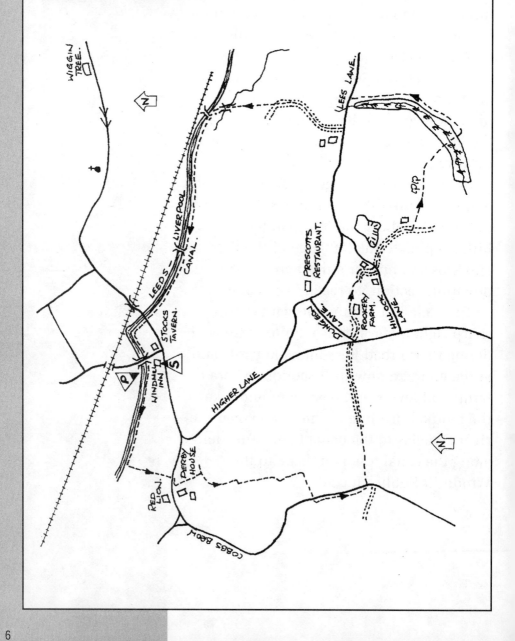

**C**ross over the canal bridge and turn left onto the canal bank. Follow the canal tow path West via Ring o' Bells, to Rufford Branch canal at Burscough.

Turn right along the Rufford Branch tow-path behind the Ship Inn, for approximately 1.5 miles to Prescotts Bridge. This will be the third bridge that you come to.

Turn right off the tow-path along Meadow Lane for 500 yards and go straight on along the footpath where the road swings to the right (ignore earlier Public Footpath sign on the left).

Follow the footpath straight ahead over stiles, and in parts, through rough undergrowth to Wood Lane. Follow Wood Lane to Wane Blades road.

Turn right and then first left along Deans Lane, over a level crossing to the canal bridge.

Turn left and follow the tow-path back to the car park.

# WALK 2
# The
# Windmill
# to
# Prescotts
# Bridge

Walk covered by:-
PATHFINDER MAP
No. 699

Start:-
MAP REFERENCE
491105
THE WINDMILL P.H.
Next to the canal.

Parking:-
Parbold side of the
canal bank.

Time of Walk:-
Approx 3.5 hrs

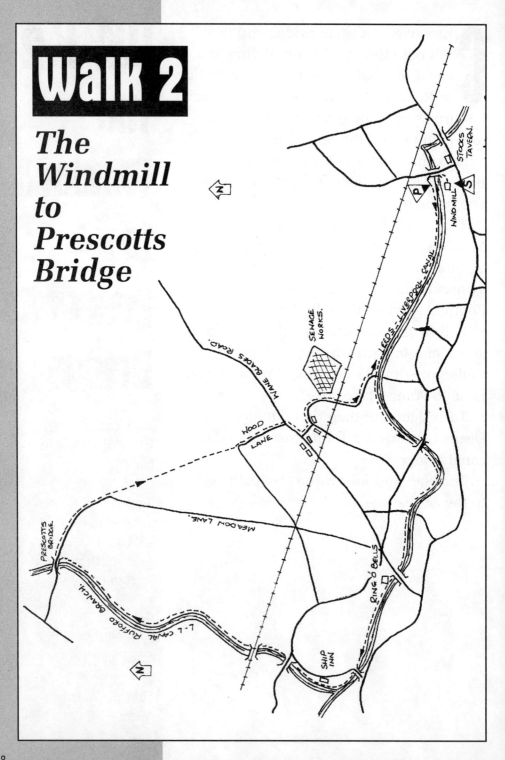

# Walk 2

## *The Windmill to Prescotts Bridge*

N

STOCKS TAVERN.

P S

WINDMILL

LEEDS - LIVERPOOL CANAL

SEWAGE WORKS.

WANE BLAKES ROAD.

WOOD LANE

MEADOW LANE.

PRESCOTTS BRIDGE

L-L CANAL RUFFORD BRANCH.

RING O BELLS

SHIP INN

N

Cross over the canal bridge and follow the road over a level crossing, passing Parbold Library on the right. Continue round the bend and slightly uphill for 150 yards then take the footpath on the left between the houses. Follow the path down to a stile.

Cross the stile and turn right. Follow the footpath straight ahead for 1 mile to reach Hall Lane (take care emerging on to the road here). Turn right along Hall Lane to reach Grimshaw Green.

Turn left into Grimshaw Green Lane and after approx 500 yards, take the footpath on the right over the football field and the children's playground to Chorley Road. Turn right towards Hilldale Post Office and then turn left up Hillside Avenue, this soon deteriorates into an unmetalled track, follow this up to the entrance gates of the Old Quarry.

Take the footpath which skirts the right edge of the quarry to a stile. Cross the stile and go uphill to a stile in the left hand corner of a field. Cross the stile into Bannister Lane.

Turn right and follow the lane up to the Rigbye Arms where you then bear left along High Moor Lane for about 20 yards.

Turn right into the driveway of Stoney Bank House, after about 20 yards leave the driveway on the right to follow the path between fence and garden, through a gate

# WALK 3
# The Windmill to the Rigbye Arms

Walk covered by:-
PATHFINDER MAP
No. 699

Start:-
MAP REFERENCE
491105
THE WINDMILL P.H.
Next to the canal

Parking:-
Parbold side of the canal

Time of Walk:-
Approx 2.5 hours

to a lane. Turn right, then bear left at the farm, to continue down hill until the track becomes a footpath leading to a stile.

Continue ahead on the same bearing, to a stile at the junction of the field fence and the wood. Cross the stile and continue on, with the stream and ravine on the right, cross over stile to emerge on Parbold Hill Road.

Turn left uphill, to the bend just before the Church. Cross the road (with care) to the stile opposite and take the footpath downhill with the fence on the right to Wood Lane. Turn right and then left and continue downhill over a level crossing to the canal.

Cross the bridge and turn right along the canal tow path to the Windmill Public House.

# Walk 3

## The Windmill to the Rigbye Arms

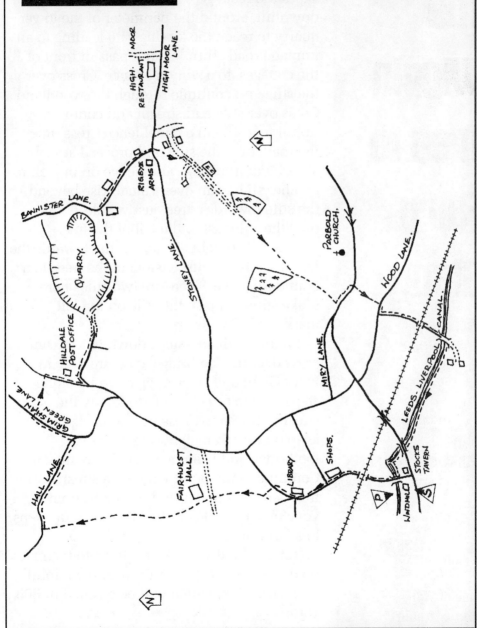

# WALK 4

# The Wiggin Tree to Fairy Glen

Walk covered by:-
PATHFINDER MAP
No. 699

Start:-
MAP REFERENCE
509107
THE WIGGIN TREE
P.H on Parbold Hill

Parking:-
Lay-by opposite the
Wiggin Tree

Time of Walk:-
Approx 1 hour

Take the downhill path, directly opposite the Wiggin Tree. Follow the path round the perimeter fence of the infill quarry and down the steps to the service road. Cross the road, go over the stile and continue downhill, around the perimeter of the lower quarry to reach the kissing gate leading to an unmade road. Turn left and pass in front of the cottages, to a stile in a fence. Cross over the stile and continue through the woodland. Cross over stile and stream and continue uphill to a stile in a panel fence.Cross over the road, over the stile and proceed straight ahead with the fence and hedge on the left to another stile. Aim over a small rise beyond the stile towards a tree, just visible. Cross over the stile just to the left of the tree.

Proceed straight ahead, aiming towards the left of the farmhouse visible in the trees to a boundary fence. There are two stiles here. Make sure you take the stile on the left marked FP.

Follow path and steps down to a stream, cross over the footbridge, (you are now in Fairy Glen) and carry straight on up stone steps. At the top turn left, to follow the stream upstream. Cross the footbridge and keep on upstream, ignoring the next footbridge and keeping to the left hand bank. Continue to the point where the stream issues from a small culvert in the bank in front of you. Take the stile on the left and go up steps to a farm track.

Turn right along the farm track to the main road. Cross the road with care and go uphill to the car park, which will be reached in 800 yards.

# Walk 4 *The Wiggin Tree to Fairy Glen*

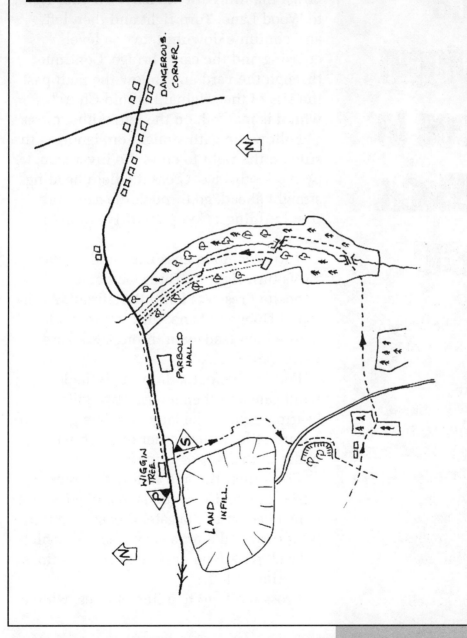

DANGEROUS. CORNER.

N

PARBOLD HALL.

WIGGIN TREE.

S

P

N

LAND INFILL.

# WALK 5

# The Wiggin Tree to Hillock Lane

Walk covered by:-
PATHFINDER MAP
No. 699 AND 711

Start:-
MAP REFERENCE
509107 MAP NO. 699
THE WIGGIN TREE P.H
on Parbold Hill

Parking:-
Lay-by opposite the
Wiggin Tree

Time of Walk:-
Approx 3 hours

From the Wiggin Tree, walk West down Parbold Hill. 50 yards past Parbold Church, cross the road with care, to the stile. Cross over this stile and continue down the hill with the fence on your right, to Wood Lane. Turn right and then left, and continue downhill, over a level crossing and the canal bridge. Continue through the yard and follow the path past the site of the original Parbold Church, which is marked, on the left, with a cross.

Follow the path straight on, ignoring the stile on the right to cross the River Douglas by the footbridge. Cross the field heading straight ahead, go through the gate and past buildings. Go up the drive to Lees Lane.

Turn left along Lees Lane and in 100 yards turn right up Dungeon Lane, opposite Prescotts Farm Restaurant. At the top of Dungeon Lane, turn left into a farm road which leads you through Rookery Farm yard.

Follow the footpath through the left hand gate and then go over two stiles, bearing right at the large tree in a gully, to a third stile in the corner of a conifer hedge at the rear of a house.

Cross this stile and follow the track to Hillock Lane. Cross the lane and go over a stile adjacent to the gate. Proceed up the farm road and after a steep section, which is brick paved, go past old farm buildings to a stile on left.

Cross the field to a line of trees, which

are followed on the right to reach an area of marshy ground. Bear right over this to the far corner of the field, which is fringed by a wood.

Cross the stile and go through the wood and up a bank, to waste ground, (site of an old mine), follow the footpath left downhill, keeping to the left edge of the field, and crossing further stiles and a steep downhill section, to reach Lees Lane.

Turn left and within 140 yards, turn sharp right by a farmhouse. Follow the well defined farm road for some 500 yards and, at the end of a downhill section, where the farm road levels out, bear right and take the footpath leading to the bridge over the River Douglas, to the canal bank.

Turn left along the tow-path then right over the canal bridge. Continue up-hill over the railway bridge to a track. Cross the track and go through the kissing gate opposite. Continue uphill around Lower Parbold Quarry, to a stile. Cross the service road, up steps, over a stile and follow the path around the in-fill quarry to the lay-by opposite the Wiggin Tree.

# Walk 5 — *The Wiggin Tree to Hillock Lane*

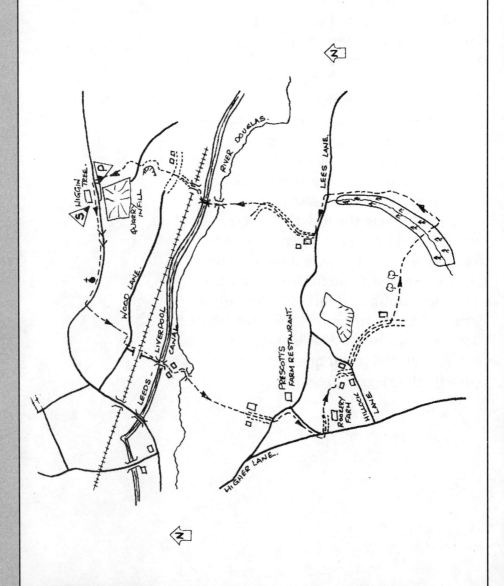

From the lay-by, just before the cottages, cross over the stone stile and go straight ahead, keeping the stream and the fence on your right.

As you get to the field corner, turn left, keeping the wall on your right, to a stile at the corner of the field.

Cross over the stile and follow the path through a small wooded area. Continue on the path, with the stream on your right, and cross two stiles, until you reach a small evergreen plantation on your left, (ignore the gate in the fence). Continue ahead, keeping the trees on your left.

Cross the ditch, and keeping to the left of the field, follow the plantation to the corner by an electricity post.

Turn left and follow the fence/hedge line past a small pond. Follow the edge of the pond and go left over a footbridge and over a stile. Keeping the hedge on the left, continue ahead under electricity lines. Follow the path along a line of electricity posts, keeping the hedge on your left, until you come to a stile. Cross the stile, and turn right to follow the track back to the main road. At the road turn left down hill to the lay-by.

# WALK 6

# Towards High Moor

Walk covered by:-
PATHFINDER MAP
No. 699

Start:-
MAP REFERENCE
516110
LAY-BY AT THE
BOTTOM OF
PARBOLD HILL

Parking:-
Lay-by at start
reference

Time of Walk:-
Approx 30 minutes

# Walk 6 *Towards High Moor*

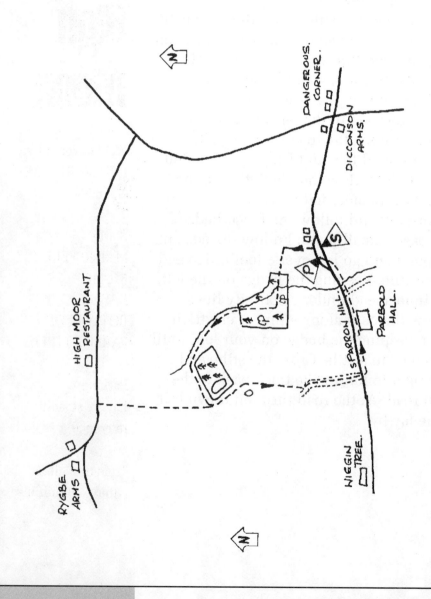

With Rigbye Arms on the left go along Bannister Lane for 600 yards. Immediately beyond the barn on the left, find the stile in the wire fence, just up from the gate. Cross over the stile and go straight ahead across the field for 70m yards to meet a broken hedge line. Turn right and follow this down hill to a stile. Cross this and follow the path through the bushes and the bracken, with the Quarry on your right.

Just before reaching the gateway at the bottom, turn sharp right and take the left hand quarry track. As you approach the summit of the hill you will see the stile on your left. Cross this and go left down the edge of the field, crossing three more stiles before entering a lane which leads to the main road.

Cross the main road and continue right for 500 yards to reach the Farmers Arms and Bispham Durnings School. Turn left immediately after the school and cross the stone stile into a field. Continue ahead along the field side and where the hedge/fence bears left, see the stile on your right.

Cross the stile and make for the farm buildings diagonally across the field. Take the stile into the bungalow garden and continue along the stream bank to the stile in the corner. Cross the stile onto the lane and turn left.

After 400 yards where the lane takes a sharp left, go right into the field and then

# WALK 7
# Rigbye Arms to Cedar Farm

Walk covered by:-
PATHFINDER MAP
No. 699

Start:- MAP
REFERENCE 508119
RIGBYE ARMS P.H.
IN HIGH MOOR

Parking:-
Adjacent to Rigbye
Arms on Stoney
Lane/Bannister Lane

Time of Walk:-
Approx 3 hours

take an immediate left (small stream on your left). Continue along the field and eventually reach a stile in the lane. Turn right and follow the lane to the junction. Turn right to Cedar Farm. Turn right again at the Public Footpath signpost. Cross the car park and go in between the fenced enclosure on the right, and the line of evergreen trees and buildings on the left.

Go over the stile at the end of the fence and turn immediately left, along the back of the buildings. At the end of the buildings, turn left and go over the stile on the the farm track and turn right. At the T junction of the tracks, turn left, then, in line with the copse on your left, go over the stile on your right and walk along the path keeping the fence on your left.

Continue ahead towards Harrock Hill, At the end of the field, go over a stile and footbridge in to a second field and continue ahead. On reaching the road, (Bentley Lane), turn left and then right, in to Jackson's Lane.

Wend your way along the lane. Ignore the first footpath sign on the left and on reaching the road intersection, turn left at the footpath sign, up the hill and past the cottages.

Continue up a driveway and across a courtyard. Go over the stone stile in the wall and continue uphill between farm buildings. Where the concrete drive turns right you continue ahead over the stile and up the grass path to the top of the field. Go ahead over two stiles, and follow the path with the fence on your left. Go over the ladder stile in the wall, then immediately right over the stile between the woodland and the wall.

Reaching an open area, and keeping the wall on the right, continue ahead to reach the stile on the right by the gate.

Cross the stile and continue ahead to the field corner, turn right along the fence line to the plantation corner. Go left up the hill towards the mast. Just before the mast, turn right over a stile and follow the path to a stile by the farm road. Go over the stile, turn left up concreted road to reach High Moor Lane, by the High Moor Restaurant. Turn right to the Rigbye Arms.

# Walk 7 *Rigbye Arms to Cedar Farm*

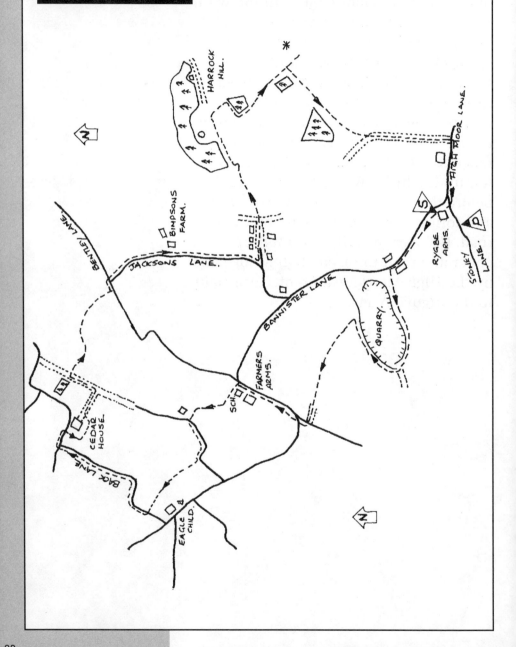

**W**alk up the concrete farm road next to the restaurant towards Harrock Hall. Over the rise, the road dips and bears left towards the Hall. Cross the stile on the right at this bend, and continue up hill on the path to reach the path junction which is by a small wood on the left. Cross the stile and turn left. Follow the path downhill to another small wood. Turn right at the corner of the wood and keeping the fence on your right walk to the field corner, and then turn left up the hill to a stile by a gate.

Cross the stile and turn right and follow the track downhill, leading to a road. Take the right fork, which is Coopers Lane, and follow the lane downhill for about a mile, to a road junction. Turn right, then left, into Town Lane. Follow the lane over a stream, going slightly up hill, with a farm on your left, to a stile on the right, next to a gate, where the road bends sharply to the left.

Cross the stile and keep straight ahead for a short distance to a fence corner. Turn left, and continue ahead with the fence on your left, past a small pond, to a stile by a gate. Cross the stile and continue, with the hedge on your right. Cross two more stiles, to reach a stile in a field corner. Cross the stile and continue ahead with the hedge on your left. Go towards some farm buildings. Follow the farm track past the front of the farm buildings, this leads into a farm road, which in turn, leads into Church Lane. At Church Lane turn right leading to Toogood Lane.

At the road junction, turn left and walk 500 yards to reach Toogood Farm, (this stretch of

# WALK 8
# Harrock
# Hill
# Circular

Walk covered by:-
PATH-FINDER MAP
699

Start:- MAP
REFERENCE
513118. HIGH
MOOR
RESTAURANT on
High Moor Lane.

Parking:-
any safe point on
High Moor Lane, or
by the Rigbye Arms.

Time of Walk:-
Approx 3 hours.

road is very busy at weekends so extra care must be taken).  Just past the farm, take the stile on the right, next to the gate.  Continue ahead along the track between the hedges and the trees to the stile.  Cross the stile and continue with the wood to your left and cross another stile.

Go straight ahead across the field to a stone footbridge and stile.  Cross the bridge and stile and go up the hill across the middle of the field to a stile in the far right hand corner by the wood.  (If crops have been planted in this field it may be easier to follow the right hand perimeter fence to the stile.)  Cross the stile, turn left to the stile leading to a sunken track. Turn left up the track for 20 yards and before you reach the gully, go right over a gate-stile and up the bank into a field.  Turn left and follow the left-hand side of the field.  Follow the bank of the gully on your left between two trees into the next field.  Where the gully ends, go left, then immediately right to follow the field track.

Continue on the track, going slightly up hill past a lone tree to a stile.  Cross the stile and continue ahead, with the hedge on your right.  Follow the obvious path down hill, over the stile by the gate, to reach the track junction.

Cross over the stile directly ahead, next to the gate.  Turn right and aim towards a small bungalow in the next field.  Cross the stile and continue towards the bungalow with the hedge on the left.  Follow the boundary of the bungalow through the wall to a farm track. Turn left on the track to reach High Moor Lane. Turn right up High Moor Lane to the High Moor Restaurant.

# Walk 8

## Harrock Hill Circular

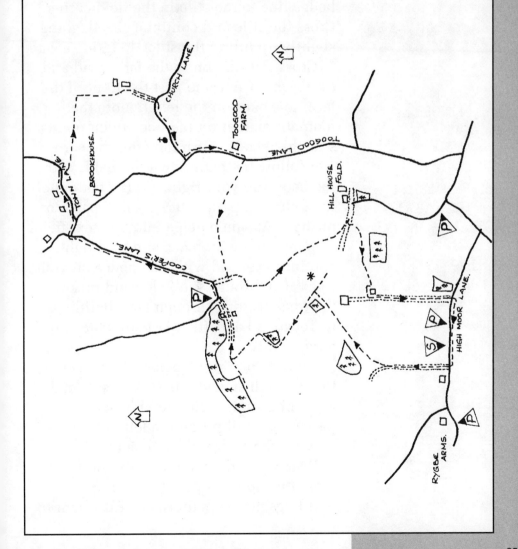

# WALK 9
# High
# Moor
# Circular

Walk covered by:-
PATH-FINDER MAP
No. 699

Start:- MAP
REFERENCE 513118.
Near HIGH MOOR
RESTAURANT

Parking:-
On High Moor Lane.

Time of Walk:-
Approx 2.25 hours.

From the High Moor Restaurant, walk down hill, to pass High Moor Farm on the right. Look for a wood on the left, with the farm road just before it. Go left up the farm road to the bungalow on the right. Go past the bungalow and enter the field behind, through a gap in the wall.

Follow the boundary fence of the bungalow to the hedge and follow the hedge line to the stile in the field corner. Cross the stile and continue ahead, going slightly up hill to the stile alongside a gate.

Cross the stile on to the farm road and turn right. Continue past the front of the farm to a barn on the left, (ignore the footpath marker on the tree which points straight ahead). Turn left after the barn and follow the path down the field, with the hedge on your right. At the bottom of the field, the path enters a small patch of bushes. As you emerge into the next field, step over the wire fence and turn right, continuing ahead with the hedge on your right. Go through the fields and pick up the track leading through farm buildings, to Toogood Lane, (this last stretch can be very muddy).

Go left, then right, before the houses at the footpath signed, 'to Mossy Lea Road'. Keep in a straight line on this path, passing a small pit on the left. Continue on with the hedge on your right.

Bear left at the bottom of the slope, cross the stile and pass between farm buildings, to the main road. Turn right to pass Mossy Lea Stores and later the Hinds Head Public House on the right.

Continue along the road for 300 yards, then turn right up the track just before the black and white arrow on the roadside. Pass through farm buildings to reach Tunley Lane. Turn right and continue to the road T junction.

Continue ahead through the gate to the right of the Toogood Lane sign and go straight ahead up a field with the hedge on your left. Go over the stile, through another field and over a bar stile to reach the farm buildings passed on the outward journey.

Pass in front of the farm and up the farm road ahead, making for the summit of the hill, and keeping the wall on your left. Pass between white Ordinance Survey Stone and mast, going alongside the wire fence on your left.

Turn left over a stile, at the end of the wire fence which precedes the woodland. Continue ahead, slightly down hill, over stiles and between trees, to reach the stile at the farm road. Cross the stile and turn left up the farm road, leading back to High Moor Lane.

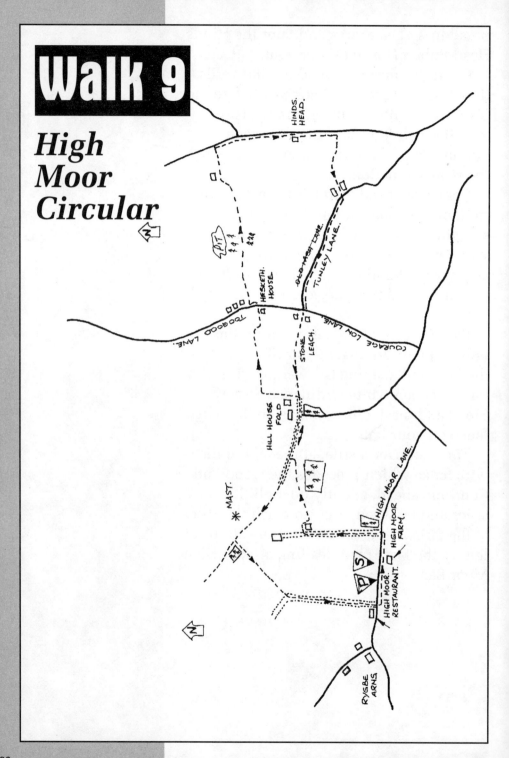

# Walk 9

## *High Moor Circular*

Start from the car park, near the school. Walk to the main road and turn right along it. (New Street). Continue through the village, keeping straight on at the crossroads, which takes you into the High Street.

Go over the wooden footbridge, on the left hand pavement, then continue up the hill and take the signed footpath on the left, 100 yards before St.Peter's Church. Follow the hedge/fence line round the graveyard to the posts on the left, and go through them.

Go over the two stiles directly ahead, then follow the hedge line, bearing right and ahead, towards the stile next to a gate. Go over the stile into School Lane and turn left. Bear left at the junction (Back Lane), and after 70 yards, go over the stile on the right, at Cedar Farm. Cross the car park and go in between the fenced enclosure on the right, and the line of evergreen trees and buildings on the left.

Go over the stile at the end of the fence and turn immediately left, along the back of the buildings. At the end of the buildings, turn left and go over the stile on the the farm track and turn right. At the T junction of the tracks, turn left, then, in line with the copse on your left, go over the stile on your right and walk along the path keeping the fence on your left.

Continue ahead towards Harrock Hill, At the end of the field, go over a stile and footbridge in to a second field and continue ahead. On reaching the road, (Bentley Lane), turn left and then right, in

Walk covered by:-
PATH-FINDER MAP 699.

Start:- MAP REFERENCE 492150 HURST GREEN SCHOOL.

Parking:- Public car park behind Hurst Green School, nr. Village Hall.

Time of walk:- Approx 3.5 hours.

to Jackson's Lane.

Wend your way along the lane. Ignore the first footpath sign on the left and on reaching the road intersection, turn left at the footpath sign, up the hill and past the cottages.

Continue up a driveway and across a courtyard. Go over the stone stile in the wall and continue uphill between farm buildings. Where the concrete drive turns right you continue ahead over the stile and up the grass path to the top of the field. Go ahead over two stiles, and follow the path with the fence on your left. Go over the ladder stile in the wall, then immediately right over the stile between the woodland and the wall.

Carry on up the hill to the old windmill. Take the path to the right of the windmill, over the crest of the hill, and take the broad path between the walls. Go down the hill, through the gate, and on to the track down to the road.

Turn left at seat and continue downhill for half a mile, then turn left at the main road. Follow the road round to the left, down a dip, then up the hill to the footpath stile on the right. Go over the stile and cross the field, keeping the hedge on your left. Go round the pond, and over the next stile.

With the hedge on your left continue ahead and then go over a third stile and turn left on to the road. Take the signed footpath on the right at Monks Farm. Go between the farm buildings and through the gate into a field. Keep close to the left hand hedge, walking along to the footbridge. Cross over the bridge and keeping the hedge still on your left, pass the pond and go over a stile, then between the properties you will reach the road. Turn left and then immediately right, over a stile.

Continue straight ahead, with the hedge on your left, and cross a second field via a small gate, still keeping the hedge on your left. Go through the gap in the corner of the field, and over the stile on your right. Continue, with the hedge on your right, through three fields, over the stile and turn left. Follow the path to the road (New Street). Turn right and retrace your steps back to the school and the car park.

# Walk 10 *Mawdesley to Harrock Hill*

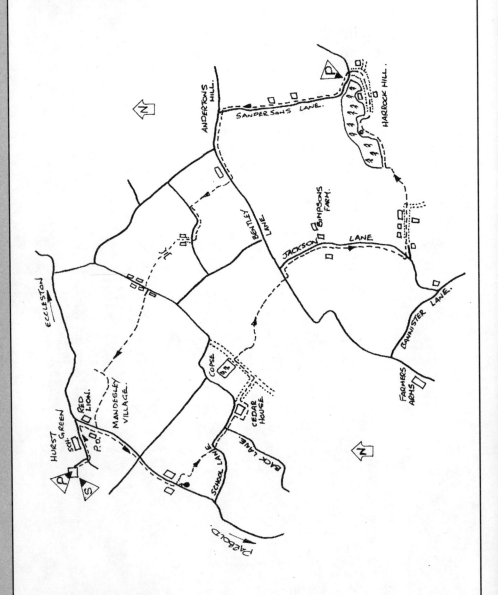

On leaving the car park, turn left and continue past the Horseshoe Inn, which will be on your left. At the T junction, turn right and then left into Whitemoss Road South and cross over the motorway bridge. Where the road turns left, you go straight ahead through the gate. (Pedestrian access is to the side of the gate).

Continue along the track, through a plantation, then cross a cinder track and head in the direction of a farmhouse in the distance. Bear left 150 yards before Rose Farm, taking the faint raised path, which leads to a gap in the hedgeline. Continue ahead, towards the house in the trees. Turn right on the track, just before reaching the house. Continue along this wide track through the farmyard at Ivy House. On reaching a surfaced road, turn left to reach the dual carriageway.

Cross over the dual carriageway to the signposted path opposite. Continue down this path for approx one mile in the direction of Bickerstaffe Church. On reaching the road, turn right, and then left at the T junction, (Hall Lane). After about 400 yards, take the farm track on the right between hawthorn hedges (approx 100 yards past the large house on the right).

Continue with the farm on your left and the wood on your right. Where the path turns left, you bear right to cross the motorway, via the footbridge. Turn left, then right over the bridge, through the trees and continue to the main road.

Cross over and continue along the road directly opposite (Long Lane). After about

# WALK 11
# The Lancashire Plain Country Walk

Walk covered by:-
PATH-FINDER MAP
No. 711

Start:- MAP
REFERENCE 461055.
HORSESHOE INN
P.H.

Parking:- Small car park near phone box.

Time of walk:-
Approx 4 hours

three quarters of a mile, turn right into High Lane and then left at the crossed tracks, towards High Lane Farm. As the track enters the farm yard, go right, with the hedge on your left, over the field to the road. On reaching the road, turn right in the direction of the water tower.

At the junction with the main road, turn right and cross over to take the track on the left, but to the right of the water tower.

At Delph Farm, go straight on between the buildings, then bear left along a fairly obvious path to Whiteley Lane, which is opposite School Lane. Turn right and proceed as far as the sharp left hand bend. Take the broad track straight ahead and where this track turns right, take the less obvious path straight ahead, but keeping to the left of the ditch.

On reaching the next hedge line, emerge into the field. Go straight ahead, taking the path which curves gradually left, this leads onto a track continuing ahead past farm buildings. On reaching the road, go directly across. Continue along the path to the right of the power lines.

Cross a graded ditch (path now narrows), and continue ahead. Keeping the tree line on your left, turn right on meeting a farm track. Pass through Holland's Farm, cross Blaguegate Moss, and where the path goes right to the farm, turn left, in the direction of a row of cottages.

Follow the path to the main road, turn left and go along to the next left hand road junction, which is Liverpool Road. Go past the Horseshoe Inn back to the car park.

# Walk 11

## *The Lancashire Plain Country Walk*

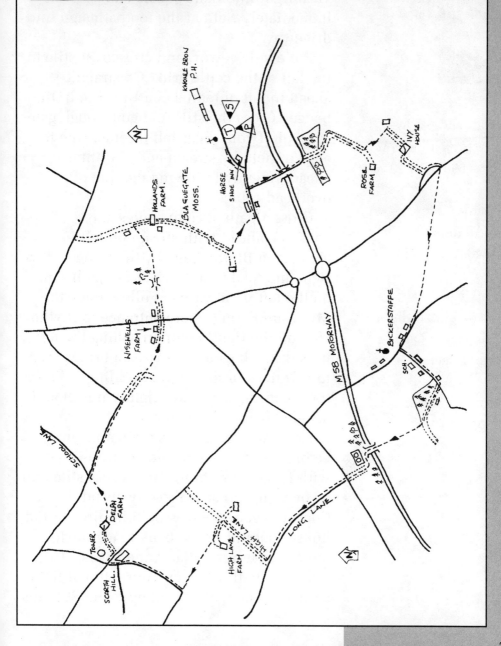

# WALK 12

# Blythe Hall

Walk covered by:-
PATH-FINDER MAPS
Nos. 699 & 711

Start:-
MAP REFERENCE
454091 Map 711

Parking:-
Start Point, layby at
entrance to Lathom
Hall Estate.

Time of walk:-
Approx 2 hrs.

Cross main road and go down Cranes Lane opposite. Continue the full length of the lane, passing the Golf Club on the left to the cross roads. Turn right into Sandy Lane and immediately right at the footpath sign into driveway.

Follow driveway, and cross over stile to the left of the cattle grid. Go straight ahead to left of tennis court to stile in the hedge. Cross the stile and go through gate in front of you. Bear left through gate to edge of field by stream and continue ahead, roughly following the line of overhead cables.

Cross a path at right angles and continue ahead with stream on left to emerge on Blythe Lane by the bridge. Turn right and take farm track at footpath sign on the left in 30 yards. Follow track to Mill Dam Farm (ignore entrance to Blythe Hall on the right) on approaching the farm, pass through gate, over stream bridge, and follow track around farm buildings. The track continues ahead, slightly uphill and cobbled over this section.

Cross stile on right at footpath sign before railway bridge and continue ahead with fence on right to stile. Cross stile and go over second stile directly ahead. Continue ahead across field in direction of houses behind raised bank to a stile, to meet path around Platt Lane Lakes. Turn right and with lakes on your left exit field corner to emerge on road opposite St Johns

Burscough Hall.

Follow track directly ahead with footpath sign.  At hedge corner, by graveyard, turn right.  Follow obvious path ahead, turning left, then right, going slightly downhill.  When level with wood corner on right, turn left along sparsely tree lined ditch to footbridge in field corner.

Cross over bridge, and keeping to left of hedge, continue ahead to emerge on to Flax Lane.  Turn right along Flax Lane to junction with Blythe Lane.  Turn right, then left in 30 yards, up driveway to Speakmans Farm.  Keep to the right hand hedge at the farm house, to small gate in the corner.

Go through gate and turn left and after approx 50 yards turn right and follow path past steel post with inverted "V" cap (pipe line marker) to farm track.  Turn right, keeping drainage ditch to your immediate right, go straight ahead to join a path coming from your right, underneath a bend in overhead power lines (this section can be very muddy when machines have been on the land).

Continue ahead in line with power lines, with hedge on right, towards Needless Inn Farm.  In front of farm, turn left along farm track to return to Cranes Lane.  Turn left and retrace your steps back to car park.

# Walk 12 *Blythe Hall*

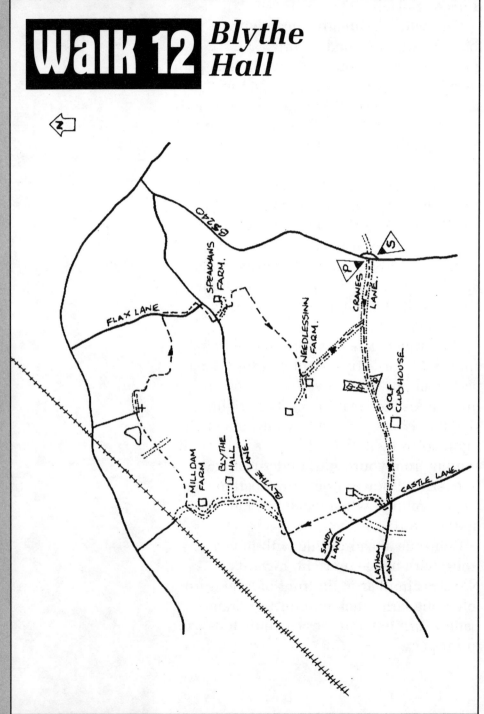

C ross main road and go down Cranes Lane opposite. Continue the full length of the lane, passing the Golf Club on the left to the cross roads. Turn left into Castle Lane and follow lane to junction with Cross Hall Brow with Halton Castle P.H. on the corner.

Turn right up Cross Hall Brow and in about 150 yards turn left at footpath sign and take track between the houses. Where track bends left by ruined barn, follow path straight ahead and continue around house garden with hedge on the left.

Follow path around corner and continue ahead down the dip, over the stream and uphill around graveyard wall to come out onto road. (St James Church, Westhead). Turn right along the road and continue for about ½ mile. Ignore the first footpath sign on the right and continue to second footpath sign by Kissing Gate at entrance to Ruff Wood.

Go through gate and follow path through wood, with hedge and wood boundary on the right. Where the path branches off to the right (quarry on the left) continue straight ahead to emerge out of wood at a stile, into an open field.

Continue straight ahead to road (Cross Hall Brow). Turn right and in 10 yards turn left down farm track sign posted Lathom Lane. Passing in front of farm buildings continue along obvious track, past pumping station to Lathom Lane.

Go straight across Lathom Lane and

# WALK 13
# Ruff
# Wood

Walk covered by:-
PATH-FINDER MAP 711

Start:-
MAP REFERENCE 454091

Parking:-
Start point, layby at entrance to Lathom Hall Estate.

Time of walk:-
2.5 hrs.

follow track to Sandy Lane. Turn left and in 10 yards turn right to follow footpath alongside stream, over stream bridge, then continue ahead in line with overhead power lines. Eventually pass through a small gate, then past a small pond and through a second small gate, to emerge onto a farm track.

Turn right along the track and pass in front of Needless Inn Farm and continue down farm track back to Cranes Lane. On reaching Cranes Lane turn left and retrace your steps back to the car park.

# Walk 13 *Ruff Wood*

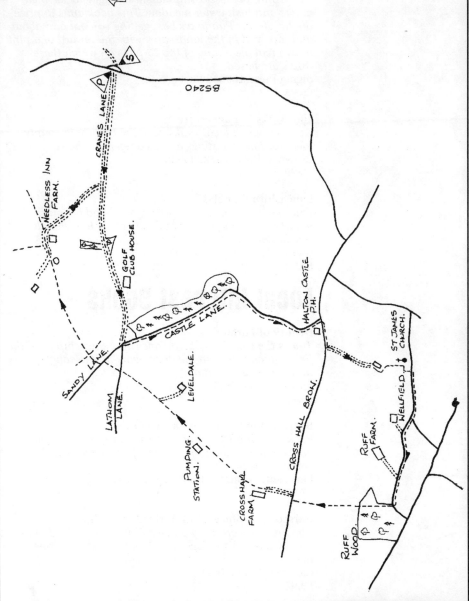

# Other Local Walking Books

### Rambles Round Mawdesley
*By Alan Cocker*
£3.99

### Pub Walks in Lancashire
*Lancashire possesses salt marshes, craggy rocks, high moors and lush water meadow. This book aims to prize the lid off this Pandora's box, getting you out and about and involved in the landscape, with the reward of a pint or two real ale at any of the 25 pubs on which these walks are based.*
Sigma Press 1850582564
£6.95

### 100 Walks in Lancashire
*An omnibus of local walks covering the whole county, ideal for family outings and as a reference book.*
Crowood Press 1852238925
£8.99

### Lancashire Rambles
*Fourteen circular walks covering wild and beautiful moorland, wooded dales and valleys such as Pendle Hill, Ribchester, Longridge Fell etc.*
Countryside Books 1853061778
£4.95

# Local Interest Books

### History of Parbold
*Traces the story of a small Lancashire township from the first reference to it in the documents of Burscough priory in the late 12th century.*
Carnegie 0948789778
£6.95

### Birdwatchers Guide to Lancashire
*Packed with information and useful tips to help the birdwatchers see all the variety of species which the country has to offer.*
Lancashire Country Books 1871236320
£7.95

### Burscough – Story of an Agricultural Village
*The life of an ordinary place and its people. England's history lies in its villages and this is the story of one of them.*
Carnegie 1859360226
£9.95